HOW TO BE MORE PRODUCTIVE IN 2021

For the last 5 years, I have been retired and writing about productivity and productivity software. I have more than 100,000 views of my articles on Medium.com and 50,000 on Newsbreak. This work was based on forty years employed in the corporate world of Information Technology and as owning several successful businesses.

Now I'd like to share some of my tips, tricks, and hacks to make you more productive in 2021.

I hope you enjoy reading these chapters and I truly hope they make for a more productive and happy life.

Darryl Brooks

See How 20 Little Seconds Changed My Life

Photo by Markus Spiske on Unsplash

A while back, I wrote a memoir piece about the road not taken and how 38 seconds changed my life.

It was a pivotal moment for me, and I will be forever grateful for the road I chose following that brief moment.

But this article isn't about a single twenty-second portion of my life. It is about a series of twenty-second periods repeated over and over.

Let me tell you how all this started.

Like many of you reading this right now on some sort of device, I spend all day, every day, looking at some kind of screen: my laptop, phone, tablet, TVs, and all the other devices that have taken over our lives. This never caused me any concern, and I never noticed my eyes getting tired or my vision worsening because of it.

The keyword here is noticed.

Then, I discovered something odd happening. If I were wandering around anywhere without focusing on something close, my eyes began to feel strained. They also began to always water when I was out and about.

It didn't worry me, but it did make me curious, so I whipped out, you guessed it, a tiny screen to research it. The research confirmed what I already assumed. That I was asking my eyes to do something they weren't accustomed to doing; focusing on things far away. It's a common problem in this modern world, and the universal solution was to train my eyes to focus near and far.

I discovered the 20/20/20 rule. What this rule simply states, (20–20 get it?), is that every 20 minutes, you spend 20 seconds staring at something 20 feet away.

Okay, that makes sense; I can do that. So I started trying to remember to take frequent breaks and look at the wall across the room.

Of course, that failed.

What are the chances that I am going to remember to tear myself away from the scintillating drivel on Twitter every twenty minutes?

Approximately zero percent.

A few weeks later, I'm wandering around Costco, happily digesting my buck-fifty hot dog, when my eyes started watering to the point that I couldn't see the price on a new screen I was contemplating. When I got home that day, I decided I needed to get serious with this 20/20/20 stuff.

I started researching timer apps.

It was then that I discovered that one of the productivity apps I am using, Amazing Marvin if you care, has a built-in Pomodoro timer. The Pomodoro method is a productivity technique using a timer, traditionally looking like a small tomato, hence the name. The idea is that you put in a dedicated period working, usually 25 minutes, then take a 5-minute break. Rinse and repeat.

If you want to learn more, read this great article by Jun Wu.

I programmed that timer for my 20/20/20 initiative. I could set the work time to 20 minutes but had to settle on wasting an entire minute on saving my eyesight. Oh drat!

So, I set the timer to repeat until I turn it off, cranked the volume on my laptop to a subtle 10%, and went to work.

Twenty minutes later, ding!

I stood up, opened the blinds, and stared out the window.

For about fifteen seconds.

That's all I could stand. It was 5 am, so not much to see, but at least I was focused on the distance. But as the timer repeated, I found I was letting that fifteen seconds draw out. Finally, it became a minute. One minute that I was doing nothing.

After only a day of that, I can tell you that the results were terrific.

No more wandering around the mall, dabbing at my eyes with a napkin, looking at the world through blurry corneas. Problem solved. Tick that off my list and move on with my life.

But that's not really a life-changing event, is it? Read on.

After a few days, like Pavlov's dog, the bell would signal me to stop doing what I was doing and do something else for a minute.

It's what I discovered then, that changed my life.

So, I'm on Medium, typing away at the next brilliant sen — Ding!

I fought every instinct I have not to finish the sentence, just stand up and turn to the window.

First, I thought, I can't believe I'm doing this. What's wrong with just finishing the sentence and then standing up? You know what's wrong with it. If I finish the sentence, I'm going to want to finish the paragraph. And then the story.

And sometime soon after that, I would silence that damned bell forever.

But I didn't do that. I turned and stared out the window. My neighbor was walking his dog, Bernie, in case you are wondering.

A few seconds after the physical bell rang, the metaphorical bell went off.

I realized I'm not doing brain surgery here. Nothing I am working on is so damned urgent that I can't take one out of twenty minutes and do something good for myself. I wasted an hour this morning scrolling through Facebook; I can't afford to lose three minutes of that hour, not looking at a screen?

It was then that I began using that minute doing other things. Thinking up the idea to write this article, for instance. Doing deep breathing, another habit I have been trying to develop, or just thinking. That's not so bad, is it?

After a week or so, I began to look forward to my little breaks. Occasionally, I find myself checking the timer to see how long before my next minute of reflection.

And here come the life-changing parts. I find that I am more productive. I turn away from the window when the one minute bell goes off, and do a brain dump of all the ideas that just pumped through my head. I also am learning to be a much more patient person. I discovered that nothing I am doing at any time of the day is so important, I can't afford to wait just a minute.

The red light will change in a minute. The queue will start moving in just a minute.

I discovered dozens of moments all through the day when I am forced to wait a minute on something. And instead of getting pissed and impatient, I use that minute to breathe, to reflect, or just be.

I'm glad you finished this article, and I hope you found it useful, educational, or entertaining.

Now stand up and look out the window.

Just twenty seconds.

Quit Getting Things Done and Get Things Done

Stop planning what to do and just do it

Photo by Yukie Emiko on Unsplash

This week I am changing my task management application. I would tell you what I am changing from and to, but that's not what this is about. I don't want you to follow me to a new platform. I want you to use the one you have. I want you to stop spending all your time planning what to do and actually do something.

Instead of telling you which app I am moving to, I could tell you the ones I've used in the past, but that would be a pretty big list. In fact, it would include every task management application ever devised that wasn't an Apple-only product. And if you went back far enough, to my Apple IIe days, it would include one of those.

I could also explain to you why I am changing. I discovered a particular need in my workflow that the old system didn't handle, but this one did. That is a good reason to change. And I came up with something that fits that description.

But it would also be crap.

The reason I am changing is the reason I have always changed; Shiny New Toy Syndrome. But that doesn't quite fit the bill either, because I am moving from my second iteration on the last app to my third iteration on this one. So, the toy isn't that shiny and it's certainly not new. But this time, it will be different. I promise. This time, I'll stick with this one.

Yeah, right?

A month, six months, a year from now, I will read or see something that will make me think about another app. And I'll probably jump ship. I hope not, but I've learned better.

So, why do I keep switching? Sometimes, I've changed my primary job and sometimes, I've changed my marketing plan. But mostly, I don't know why I switched. I'm sure there is some deeply rooted psychological issue that makes me change task management systems on a whim. Hopefully, it's a new, wildly popular syndrome with a catchy acronym.

But that is not what I wanted to talk about. Based on my experience, I want to help you be more productive. I'm not pitching a particular piece of software or a method. I don't want to talk to you about Getting Things Done, but about getting things done.

Like most everyone, at some point, I got on David Allen's bandwagon and followed the GTD method. But partway through that period is when I first discovered the problem with most productivity methodologies. They were more about following the protocols than actually doing things. I know that wasn't the intention, but in talking to people, that's how it ended up being done.

I remember being on a forum dedicated to GTD, and we were discussing how we implemented the program. I mentioned that I had fine-tuned my system to where I didn't have to do a weekly review. I only did reviews every two or three weeks.

THAT'S NOT GTD! some woman shouted on the forum. You have to do weekly reviews. Weekly reviews are what it says in GTD. Yeah, and Judge Wapner's at five. That's when I left the forum, and soon after switched away from GTD. I don't remember what. Maybe the P.A.R.A. method or BASB. I'm pretty sure it was something with a lot of letters in it.

Sometimes, we don't realize what we are doing until we watch someone else doing the same thing. Long before GTD, I was deeply involved with Microsoft Project. Wow, that was a box of Tinkertoys, wasn't it? Dependencies and Gantt Charts and, oh my, a Critical Path. I was devising a social media marketing plan back in the early days. I spent many hours plugging in all the tasks and resources and dependencies, watching the bars on that Gantt Chart grow and shrink.

Another manager stopped by to check out what I was doing and told me she could use that for a project of hers. She bought a copy and was off to the races. A week later, she called me into her office to help her with a section of the project. It had about a million rows in it.

Then I looked at the Gantt chart. It spanned two days. She had spent a week tediously outlining tasks and resources for a project that she could have finished last Tuesday.

Then I realized I was doing the same thing. Spending 40 hours planning a 16-hour job.

I've watched myself go from one extreme to the other over the years. For a while, I used Outlook as my all-in-one tool, and it is very good at that. But it had one weakness shared by many others. It only has three of four levels of priority. I was working then and wanted much finer control over priorities. I wanted to know precisely what's next, and nothing else, but I couldn't do that with four priorities.

So I invented my own. I discovered a field called percent done, I could put it on the to-do list and sort by it. Hallelujah! I now had, count 'em, 100 priority levels. And I used them all.

Now that I am retired, I'll swing back in the other direction. At various times, I'll delete my current to-do app and go for several days with no list at all. I know, crazy, right? I get a little twitchy, but I get through it. And what I discover is, nothing bad happened. I didn't even forget to take out the trash.

So, I load up one of the simpler, more basic task management tools and start over. I only load the time-sensitive tasks and the items that I absolutely don't want to forget.

And that works for a while. Then I add things and more things on top of that. Soon, brush my teeth is on the list and I know I've gone over the top again.

Don't get me wrong. Done right, any of these tools and methods will work. Millions of people have turned their lives around following David Allen, or my early hero, Ken Blanchard, of One Minute Manager fame. But there are too many like me that get bogged down in minutiae or believe the method is more important than results.

So, here is what I want you to try. First, we will break down your old system and then build a new one. Let me be clear, I don't want you to change applications or methodologies. If you are following GTD using Todoist, then stick with that. If you still have your Daytimer binder from 1985, keep at it. Only if a clean slate will help you achieve a result, do I want you to change. We can adapt any method to this one, or vice versa. Just remember, it's the goals, not the methods.

Print out your entire task list, from everything you have on for today, through that thing you noted for 2050. Next, go through the list and scratch out everything you don't need reminding of. I know it's nice checking things off, but the first two things on your list shouldn't be wake up and get out of bed. Delete the crap.

Next delete everything you have been dragging along day to day for weeks, if not months. You didn't clean out the garage last month or yesterday, and you probably will not do it today. If any of these things actually become pressing, you can add them back in,

Now, take one last look, and do a final cleansing. Everything on it should be something you need to do, will do and need reminding of it, or it's part of a larger project that you are actively working on.

What's left is your actual task list. If you are like me, it's probably about one-third of the original.

Now, let's build a simple and sustainable method for going forward. I don't have a spiffy acronym, but I will borrow from most of the other systems out there.

Your new process needs five buckets: inbox, task list, projects, someday and reference. Put your newly cleaned to-do list in the task bucket. Give yourself a reasonable timeline and use priorities that make sense to how you work.

For me, I don't set priorities according to importance or urgency, but when I will do it. There are things I do first thing because that's when it makes sense to me. I like to schedule all of my marketing posts before 6 am. It's not the most urgent or important thing I will do all day, but I don't have to think about it again.

You do you. But make sure it is doable and sustainable. Look at today and tomorrow. Are you really going to do all that? If not, fix it.

Put nothing into your inbox now, but set up methods for getting stuff there. This is the digital version of the old wooden inbox that used to be on everyone's desk. Everything that was yours got tossed in there. But don't be the guy that lets it just pile up until it falls onto the floor.

Devise a method to get every email, note, and idea quickly and easily into that inbox. The beauty behind GTD and other successful productivity methods is you don't have to remember things. Everything gets dumped into the inbox immediately, unless:

It's a waste of time, in which case you delete it.

It takes less time to do than process, in which case you do it.

Every day, at least once a day, clean out the inbox. Completely. Don't leave so much as a paper clip in it. First, pass it back through the above two filters. Do it or delete it. Everything left is either a task, project, reference material, or something you want to do someday. In which case, you put it in the appropriate bucket.

Someday and reference are for things you may need to get back to. Cleaning out the garage goes into the someday bucket. Look through it every once in awhile and see if there's something you want to pull out and deal with. Reference is just that. Information you want to keep for future reference.

Projects is a kind of temporary inbox. And I mean temporary. At least once a week, or more often if necessary, pull out any project and break it down into tasks. Add those tasks to your task list. This may take a few minutes or a few hours but is worth it. Something as complex as creating a multi-site social media marketing campaign becomes a task on today's list called Tweet a link to my new article.

That's it. Keep it simple, maintain it daily, and make sure it's working.

Now, if you'll excuse me, I'm supposed to clean out the garage. If you need me, I'll be on the couch.

What Do You Do If You Don't Have a Plan?

How Do You Get Where You're Going?

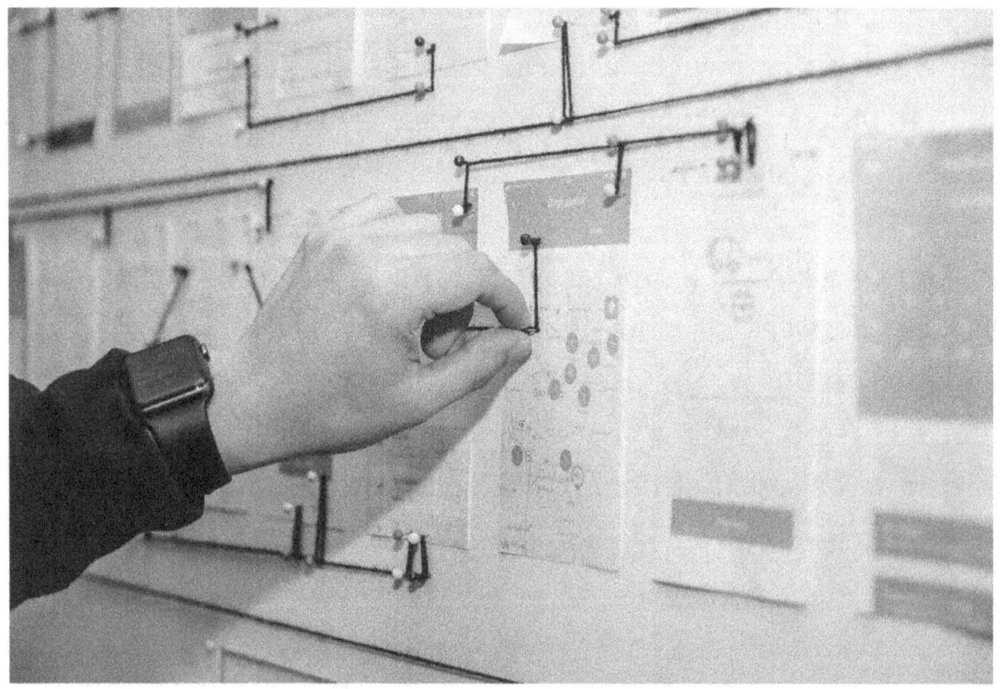

Photo by Alvaro Reyes on Unsplash

Do you know that job interview question, "Where do you see yourself in five years?"

Nobody ever asked me that.

Which is a good thing. I read about it in some article on how to prepare for an interview. And I thought about it. But I couldn't come up with an answer that didn't sound like complete bullshit. Maybe that's what they want to hear; I don't know. Fortunately, I never had to find out.

I don't know if it was the times I grew up in, the sixties and seventies, or the times have changed. Or maybe it's just me. It seems like I never had a plan, and I didn't know anyone else who had one either. Of course, I didn't exactly choose the cream of the crop to hang around with.

But today, it seems like every kid you talk to has their whole life mapped out. At least through college and beyond. The only time in high school I ever thought about college, was when they made me take some sort of test. It wasn't the SAT; you actually had to want to take that one.

Whatever test it was didn't spark a rash of college recruiters knocking on my door.

Don't get me wrong; I was never lazy. I started working when I was thirteen. Forty hours at a buck thirty-five was a fortune. I had discovered Nirvana. I never didn't want to work after that. And I've never not worked. Fifty-two years later, fully retired, and I work at my writing and photography every day.

Every day.

But I still didn't have a plan. Bussing tables at HoJos, I never thought about a career path that would lead me to be a manager. I just showed up every day and worked.

And every day after that.

Every day.

But without a plan. I hardly ever even looked for a job. They always sort of just fell into my lap.

Did you ever just go for a drive? You hear about that all the time, but I don't know anyone who actually does it. I mean just get in the car and go with no destination in mind. Most people, even if they are 'just going for a drive,' have a plan. We'll head north to the Blue Ridge Parkway, have lunch in Asheville, and then...

They have a plan.

I used to do this all the time when I was single. Just jump into my old Volkswagon and go. Sooner or later, I ended up back at home. Even years later, I used to do it with my camera and motorcycle. I just took off and rode in random directions. When I saw something I wanted to take a picture of, I put down my feet, picked up the camera, and snapped a shot. When I got tired, I turned on the old, clunky first-gen GPS on my handlebars and told it to take me home.

It usually did.

It turns out, I am not alone. Most people don't have a plan. In a survey released by DHM Research in Portland, Oregon, two-thirds of Americans don't have a plan. I know it's easy to fall into that trap. You face every day as it comes and deal with what happens. Tomorrow will take care of itself.

But will it? At some point, you will wake up and there won't be a boss telling you what to do today. Are you ready for that? Apparently, 66% of us aren't. And then it's too late.

"Write, Open, Act: An Intentional Life Planning Workbook" is a few years old, but still a great tool to plot your life. I have written here about how to figure out when and if you have enough money. If nothing else, you need to plan that far.

Another great resource I have been following lately is August Bradley. I am currently using his advice to help plan my Notion databases, but his ideas on how to plan and organize your life are very thorough and thought-provoking. He uses a system similar to Tiago Forte's P.A.R.A. method called Pillars, Pipelines, and Vaults in his Notion setup, but it is his Pillars concept that resonated with me. I wish I had seen it sooner.

Maybe I would have had a plan. Or at least a framework in which to create one.

But, I know how you feel and understand your lack of a plan, or maybe even a lack of desire to have one. I didn't have one for years, decades even.

So, how did I end up here? Retired in a nice house in a nice neighborhood with a nice chunk of change to get me through to the end?

I wrote in another <u>article</u> that if you wanted to get better at something, find someone who is better than you and hang around them.

So, since I apparently wasn't so good at this whole life thing, I found someone smarter than me.

And married her.

She had the plan. She always had a plan. When I met her, she had just put down a deposit on her first house, later our first house. I didn't know anybody that didn't live in an apartment. But she had a plan.

And eventually, that plan became my plan. As we divided up areas of responsibility, she took over the big picture, long-term investments, and strategies, while I took the day to day, nuts and bolts of paying bills etc.

And, once we reached a certain point, since I was familiar with the short term income and expenses, (and I was the spreadsheet geek), I created our plan for retirement. And, I can tell you, knowing that right now, today, you have enough to retire, is a very liberating piece of knowledge.

But, without that plan, you have nothing, but hopes and dreams.

So, what do you do if you don't have a plan? How do you get where you're going?

Hell if I know.

Let me go ask my wife.

Before You Shut Down for the Day, Do These Things

And Make Tomorrow Better

Photo by Francesco Ungaro on Unsplash

Do you want to make tomorrow a better day before it even begins?

Then it would be best if you started today before you shut down for the day.

I know how you feel. It's the end of the day; you're tired and cranky. It's been a tough day, and you've done all you can do. Whatever is left can wait until tomorrow.

So you close your laptop or put your computer to sleep and walk away.

But there are two major problems with that. Today and Tomorrow.

Today didn't suddenly get better because you left work unless you are one of the lucky ones that can just turn off your brain. I am like that. I can shut down my mind and forget about stuff until the next day.

Except when I can't. And my eyes pop open at 3 am with things left undone or waiting for me hit me in the head and ruin my sleep. It doesn't happen often, but why leave it to chance.

And tomorrow won't be any better than today. You will wake up with that anxious feeling in your gut, dreading what you know is lurking in the office. Or worse, that nagging fear of the unknown. You don't know what will spring at you as you walk in the office.

But in a half-hour at the most, you can fix all of that. And with practice, you can reduce that time to twenty or even ten minutes. You can leave the office clear of mind and be ready to hit the ground running in the morning.

Review Your Day

First, take a quick look at the day you are finishing up. What went wrong? How could you have done things differently? What went right? How can you replicate that success? What didn't get finished, and how does that fit into your plan for tomorrow?

Clear the Decks

Put away all paperwork on your desk. File it, throw it away, or put it back in your inbox. But don't get lazy with that last part. The stuff in your inbox is either those things you didn't get to review today or are associated with your very first tasks in the morning.

Save all work on your computer and shut down every app. There is nothing so distracting as waking up your system in the morning and be faced with dozens of windows and tabs. You haven't done anything, and you are already scattered all over the place.

Process your email inbox. If there is anything left in your inbox, deal with it. Typically, if it is something really quick, you would do it now, but there's no time for that unless it is a swift reply that will put the item to rest.

Everything else either gets filed for future reference or becomes part of…

Plan Your Morning

You can plan your whole day if you want, but I want you to plan your morning for this exercise. Based on your review of the day and things left undone, and the processing of your inboxes, plan your morning. It may be as little as the first hour or two, but know what you need to do first and schedule those things.

You know you are probably going to grab a coffee or tea, then check your emails — the things you always do first thing, but then, what's next. Go ahead and plan that first thing you are going to tackle. Of course, emergencies do happen, and your morning email may change this, but we let that happen far more often than it actually needs to.

Pick your unfinished task for today or your most important task for tomorrow and put that high on your task list. If nothing is genuinely pressing, plan that thing you have been putting off the longest. Swallow the frog.

Knowing what your first task will be in the morning will make your evening, and tomorrow, much better.

Once you review your day, clear the decks and plan your morning, you can leave the office with a clear mind and have clarity for tomorrow. Best of all, since you know exactly what you will be doing first thing, tomorrow holds no fear, uncertainty, or doubt.

You can now switch your focus to home and family where it belongs.

But first, take a moment and breathe. Relax your mind and body. Then walk out of the office with your head held high and a smile on your face.

If nothing else, it will make your coworkers wonder what you're up to.

How to Prepare to Get More Things Done

Do this before you work so you can work better

Photo by Piotr Wilk on Unsplash

In the American south, there is a colloquialism; fixing, usually pronounced without the G sound, as in fixin'. It means you are about to do something. Some people mistake it for a synonym of preparing, but it is more of preparing to prepare. You are about to do something, but you have done nothing yet. Or, as they would say, you ain't done nothing yet. I'm fixin' to cook dinner. I'm fixin' to go to the store.

I'm fixin' to get to work.

And that's what I want to talk to you about today, and I promise I'll leave the jargon behind soon. I want to talk to you about the work you do so you can get to work and get more things done. Part of it is traditional preparation, and part of it is the mental gearing up, similar to fixin'.

So, let's get to it.

For many people, the span between not working and working is the time to sit down behind a desk. One minute they're not working, the next they are. And if you are just coming back from a break, which I highly recommend, that may be okay; we'll get back to that in a minute.

I'm talking about when you first prepare to start work in the morning, or whenever you begin your work period. Just like I've described in my morning routine and end-of-day routine, linked below, I want you to develop a routine to begin working and to end working. I promise you, it will help you get more done and in a less stressful manner.

So preparing you to begin your workday, I first need to cover the end of the day. How you leave your workspace when you quit work will determine what state it is in when you begin. This will be very hard for some of you, but if you practice it, like any other skill, you will master it.

You know who you are. You sit down to your computer, which has 18 programs running, including at least one browser with 47 tabs open. You have to move a pile of papers off of your keyboard to do anything, so you place that pile on the larger stack next to the monitor. You brush the crumbs off your mouse pad and begin clicking away, trying to get to where you need to start.

Your desk is cluttered, your mind is cluttered, and you are getting off to a terrible start.

End your day

So, I want you to end your day like this. Scan your email. More on that process in the Begin the day section. Go through your task management software; again covered later. Close every tab in your browser. If you need to remember where you were, that's what bookmarks are for. Close the browser and every other program that is running. This next step will be the most difficult, but it is essential for success. Ready?

Shut down your computer.

That's right; just shut it down. I know you haven't done this voluntarily since you bought the thing, but it will make this process so much better. In addition, it will clear your computer's memory, so when you start tomorrow, your computer will run much faster.

Next, clear everything off your desk. There will be a future article about going paperless, but let's not try to do too much at one time. Baby steps. Organize every piece of paper into functional areas and file them away.

In a drawer.

Out of sight.

Declutter

The first day, you need to schedule some time to do this. Maybe half a day. But the effort will be worth it. You will discover a lot of paper you don't need anymore, so trash it. You will find paper that didn't need to be paper; printouts of websites you can easily bring up on the computer. There will be papers for projects, you haven't touched in weeks, if not months. Create a file and put them away. Make yourself a note to add something to your task management system (You do have one don't you) for future reference. Finally, create files and put away current projects and tasks.

Look! There's your desk. It's beautiful, isn't it?

Continue by putting everything else away. Ideally, what I'd like you to see is your laptop or keyboard, a monitor (or two), and your mouse. At most, a notepad and pen. That's it.

And that's how I want you to end each day. Desk clean and computer off. Now you are ready to begin a new day.

Begin the day

Before you get to your desk, I want you to have followed your morning routine. Breathe and stretch. Eat and have some coffee. Exercise. Breathe and stretch again.

When you get to your desk, you are relaxed, with a clear mind and ready to work.

Sit down at your desk and just think for a few minutes. Let your mind wander. Because of where you are and how you ended the previous day, your mind will eventually focus on work. It's inevitable. It's what you're there to do.

But by just sitting a few moments first, your mind achieves clarity. It also allows you to get ready to work, so that starting work is the logical next step and your mind goes there unbidden, rather than you having to drag it there kicking and screaming.

Now. It's time. Turn on the computer.

When it boots up, I want you to do three things. The order doesn't matter, but I want you to do them in the same order every day.

- Scan your social media

- Scan your email

- Look at your task management and calendar software.

Social Media

You will do it, so you may as well incorporate it into your schedule and get it out of the way. But set a timer. Ten to twenty minutes. That should get your fix in. Then, close those tabs and turn off social media notifications unless your job depends on them. Later, when you take a break, you can check again.

Email

You can find hundreds of articles on inbox zero, so I don't want to go into details here. But you will have gone through the same process at the end of the day, so you are only seeing emails that came in overnight. Delete the trash. Schedule and file the things you need to do later. Answer or handle anything that you can do in less than 2 minutes. Inbox Zero.

Task Management

Again, there is plenty of information out there about how to manage your tasks, along with many methodologies for handling them. But whatever method you use, use it. You can do this at the end of the day or the beginning, but do it at the same time every day. Look at what didn't get finished yesterday and reschedule it. Check your priorities and make sure everything is in order. Schedule tasks from your email and calendar. Before you begin work, you need to know what to work on and in what order.

Now, your mind is clear, your desk is clear, and you have your direction plotted for the day. It's time to get to work. For some of you, these habits will be tough but stick with them. They will pay off. End your day clearing your slate and begin each day with a clean one.

But there is one more subject I wanted to talk about and that is taking breaks.

Take breaks

Take them. Lots of them. Short ones and long ones. Schedule them and prioritize them so they don't get left behind. They are as important as the other tasks, so treat them that way.

I suggest taking tiny breaks, one minute or less, two to three times an hour. For those, leave your desk as is. But I also suggest taking longer breaks periodically and at least a one hour, preferably two hour, break at mid-day.

For those, follow a mini version of your end of day routine. Anything that is finished, close it, and put it away. Anything you are still working on, organize it, and make sure you have it in the right priority. Also use the longer breaks to check email and social media.

Now, if you'll excuse me, it's the end of my day.

How to Do a Weekly Review to Increase Your Productivity

Evaluate what is working well and what isn't.

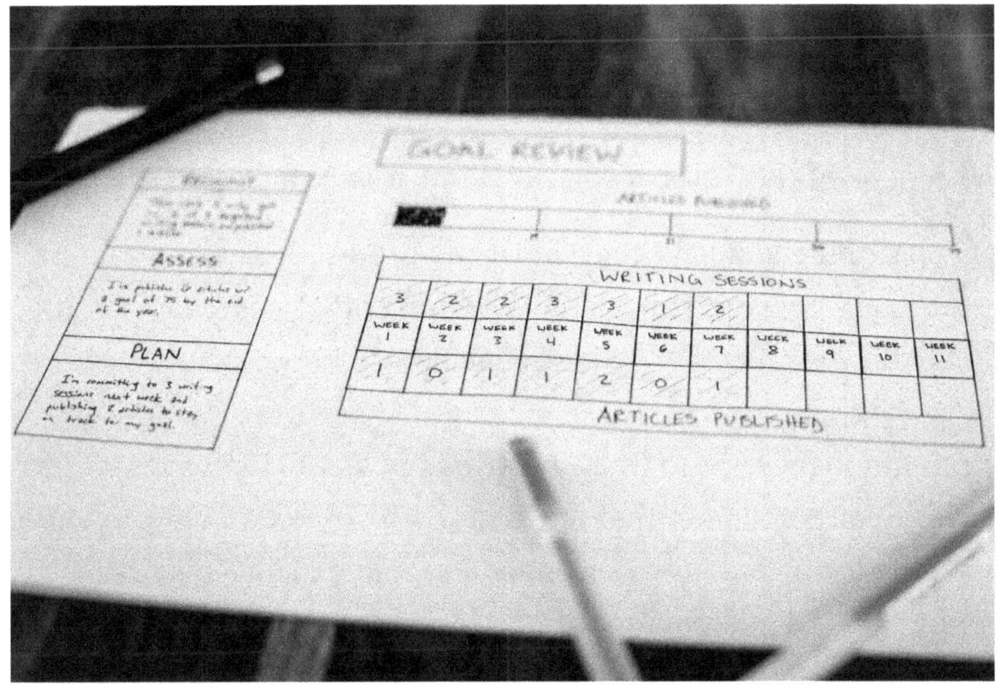

Photo by Isaac Smith on Unsplash

My weekly review used to go like this. Bring up my task management software and switch to a weekly view. Yep, got stuff to do in all seven days. Check. Done.

Like many things on my to-do list, the weekly review had become something to do by rote, simply to have something to check off the list. I almost deleted it as it had become useless, but then rethought the process.

Weekly reviews represent an essential step in productivity. Rather than delete it, why don't I improve it and do it right?

So that is what I did, and it's made a massive difference in my weekly productivity.

What a Weekly Review Is and What It Is Not

The first thing you have to do with any project or task is to define it. After all, how can you check something off as complete if you don't know what complete looks like?

First, I thought back to when I started my system and did my first review. You remember that one. It's when you set down your short and long term goals and objectives and mapped out this comprehensive plan for your life. Whew, that was a chore, wasn't it?

It's not that.

You don't need to evaluate each plan and goal on your project management list. That's a different job. This is a 'weekly' review.

Sure, you need to glance through your project list and make sure nothing has fallen through the cracks, but you are only looking at the next seven days, not your entire life. No wonder you fluffed it off.

A weekly review should just consist of the following steps:

- Review Last Week

- Scan Projects and Goals

- Check Inputs

- Plan Week

Review Last Week

The first thing you need to do on a weekly review, and this is the step most people skip, is to review the previous week. This isn't just to see what didn't get done, although that's part of it, but how did it go in general. Were you overwhelmed? Did a lot of stuff not get done, simply because you had too much to do? Did things get bumped or missed because there were too many unplanned interruptions?

Before you can plan the next week, review the previous week. Otherwise, you'll just be making the same mistakes over again. If you had twenty things on last Monday's list, you'd put twenty things on this Monday's list, even though you only got to half of them.

Don't do that.

The flip side of that is if last week went fine; if you met your goals and objectives and checked everything off your list, leave well enough alone. If it ain't broke, don't fix it. If it's working for you, keep doing the same thing.

After reviewing the previous week and determining what, if anything, needs to be changed, it's time to tackle next week. You aren't starting from scratch each week. Most of what follows may already be on your next week's list, but you need to get into the habit of going through the process each week to make sure.

Scan Projects and Goals

This is the part many people get bogged down in and why the weekly review falls apart. If your system isn't set up so that you can quickly scan your projects and goals and see what you have done and what you need to do next, then that system needs work. Maybe redesigning your project management system needs to be a new project.

If your system is working correctly, you will be able to quickly identify what items need to be done next, including any dependencies that have to be cleared first. Check your task list for the coming week and make sure each item is on there in the right order. Add any that are not and rearrange those that are in the wrong order. Make sure as you shift unfinished tasks from last week, that you don't overload next week. That will just compound the problem.

Check Inputs

This is a vital part of the weekly review, but if done right and regularly will just become a habit that takes no more than five minutes. Scan all of your inputs for random things that popped up and need addressing and adding to your weekly schedule. Inputs include:

- Email — There should be a folder devoted to these things; don't just leave them in your inbox.

- Note Taking App(s) — You should have dedicated apps to grab notes, screenshots, etc. for later reference. Limit how many of these you have to go through. There may be one more comprehensive like Evernote, and one that is more on-the-fly, like a memo pad in your task management software.

- Calendar — Notice this isn't plural. You should only have one. If you need separation, i.e., business and personal, use colors or other differentiators. You don't want your time-based tasks scattered all over the place. Do a quick review — an appointment you added six months ago is easy to forget about.

If you have more places than these for your day to day inputs, you need to consolidate. It's fine to jot notes on a sticky or notepad, but transfer them to your note-taking app daily. Stick to inbox zero, so your email is efficiently organized, and you are only looking in one place for future to-dos. Consolidate your calendars, but don't overcomplicate them. Anything that isn't tied to a particular day and time shouldn't be on the schedule.

Plan the Week

Now you've done all the hard work. You have a week that is probably at least partially planned and a list of things that need to be on it. Now it's just a matter of putting everything on your task list, making sure of two crucial points. Make sure everything is in the proper order. Double-check dependencies and things that are waiting on someone else.

And more importantly, ensure that you aren't overloaded. You know how much you can do. There is no point in adding too many things to each day just because you think they all have to get done. There is great satisfaction in checking the last item off the list before the day is done. Ending each day with unfinished tasks leads to frustration.

Also, include breaks, fun, and exercise. All work and no play makes you tired and ineffective. Take tiny breaks often. Take longer breaks as needed. Take one break of an hour or two in the middle of the day. This can be when you schedule your exercise, which is also essential. You may think padding your schedule with all of this not working stuff will slow you down, but in the long run, your productivity will improve.

Plan a weekly review at the same time each week and stick to it. With practice, it won't take more than thirty minutes. If it takes longer, you need to revisit your whole process. If it gets done in five minutes, you're not doing it right.

Now, I can check writing this article off my list.

What's next?

Start Your Day off Right

You set the tone for your whole day the moment you wake up

Photo by Lauren Kay on Unsplash

A day that begins well tends to stay on track. But if you are the type that drags out of bed at the last minute and hits the ground running, you are doing yourself, and your day, a disservice. Even if you are a morning person and go to the gym for an early workout, your day begins the moment you open your eyes. Follow these tips for a better morning routine.

Your morning routine starts before you even get out of bed. In fact, it begins before you even get in the bed. Leave your tablet and smartphone in another room. You'll be staring at screens all day; they can wait a few minutes. Don't get stressed before you wake up properly.

Next, do nothing. Just lie there and allow your system to come fully awake. Then do some gentle stretches. Stretch out your legs, knees, and shoulders before getting up. Roll over to a sitting position on the edge of the bed and do a few knee lifts and ankle circles. Stretch your back and rotate your head and neck.

Image by Author

Rise slowly and walk over to the windows. Open the shades and let some light into the room. Sunlight will inform your mind it's time to be up and about. Your body can also start taking in some vitamin D. If you are up before the sun, leave the shades open for when it does arise. Go ahead and open the windows to let some fresh air in, or at least, non-recycled air.

Now continue easing into the day by drinking a glass or two of water while you brew your favorite morning beverage. Sit down for a few minutes and enjoy that first cup, letting your mind wander where it will.

By the time you find yourself thinking about what you need to do today, your mind and your body will be ready to face whatever challenges the day brings, relaxed and non-stressed.

Make time for breakfast. You've always heard itself the most important meal of the day. Whether that's true or not, it is your first chance to get some fuel in your system, so why skip it. Get up 20 minutes earlier and have a quick but nutritious breakfast. Starting your day hungry will lower your energy and compound the problem by making you reach for unhealthy snacks all morning.

It doesn't matter how much you have to do today or how hectic things will get later; you don't have to jump into the deep end first thing. Take fifteen minutes first thing in the morning for yourself and another twenty for a good breakfast.

Your day will thank you.

Sooner or Later You Are Going to Have to Commit

Stop Thinking About It and Do It

Photo by Amine Rock Hoovr on Unsplash

We all ride the fence from time to time. Indecision causes inaction. We endlessly weigh the pros and cons of a decision, and the result is that no decision is made.

Should I marry this person?
Should I buy that alpaca farm?
Regular or crunchy raisin bran?

But frequently, not making a decision is worse than either of the options you are weighing. The decision gets taken out of your hands. A great opportunity passes while you flip back and forth. The store sells out of raisin bran.

At some point, you have to commit.

One method of deciding is by looking at the worst that can happen.

But that, in itself, can lead to indecision. If you focus on the downside of both options, that may delay even the simplest of choices.

When I met my future bride, we went through some of the habitation habits that many new couples do. I spent more and more time at her place but kept my apartment. Just in case. But that shows a lack of faith in your partner that can erode the relationship and become a self-fulfilling prophecy.

So one day, I had to go all in. I dumped the old place and moved the rest of my meager possessions into our first home.

And that went great. We were both happy, and I think our lives were made better by becoming a single unit. But single was the operative word, we didn't get married, even though we were a couple in every other sense.

Then one day, we went all in. Hey, let's get married. Okay. It was no big deal; we announced it to friends and family, went to the Justice of the Peace one Wednesday evening, and made it official.

Because sooner or later, you're going to have to commit.

I guess my biggest lesson in fighting indecision and making a commitment came a few years before all that. I wrote about it here.

One Saturday afternoon, I found myself sitting in the open door of a Cessna 182 with a parachute strapped to my back. The jumpmaster pats me on the back and yells, "GO!"

It was probably only about three seconds, but it felt like I sat there for a long time, thinking about that decision. It had only been about eighteen hours since some friends, and I decided to do this. That decision was made. We had been busy all morning getting to the place and cramming in a few hours of 'lessons.'

Lessons. On how to fall out of an airplane.

And as the four of us lined up at the door ready to board the plane, the jumpmaster asked who wanted to go first. My friends all took one step backward.

That decision was made.

So, I sat there and went through my what's the worst that can happen routine. That one was pretty obvious. I had studied aerodynamics and physics with Wile E. Coyote. I knew what was the worst that can happen.

But sooner or later, I had to commit. You'll have to read the other article to get to the end of that story, but spoiler alert: I lived.

As many of you know, I recently decided to take up the guitar. I thought about it for weeks, months even. I weighed the pros and cons. I researched types and models. I looked into lessons, both live and online.

But sooner or later, you have to commit. The time between me making that final decision and taking ownership of a guitar was about two hours.

Probably our most significant life decision since marriage was retirement. Now that one, we rode the fence on for years. We analyzed and agonized. Leaving that safety blanket of full-time employment we had endured for forty-five years was a tough decision, probably the toughest we ever made.

But I remember one day we were talking about it. I had run the numbers endlessly. I was getting pretty fed up with my job, and I could tell she felt the same. So after another day of thinking it through, I said to her, "I can promise you two things about retirement whether we do it now or five years from now. One, we will be okay. How do I know this? We are always okay. Two, no matter when we do it, we will wish we had done it sooner.

And within a few weeks, it was done.

Any time you are faced with a choice in life, thinking it through is always a good thing. But you can take it too far. Because you are not deciding between two options, but three. The third choice is not making a decision.

And that is rarely the best choice.

Not only do you not move forward with whatever the decision is, but the indecision also weighs on you. You may think you've put it out of your mind, but you never do. Should I or shouldn't I is always looming in the back of your mind, distracting and aggravating you. According to AIESEC (formerly known as the Association Internationale des Étudiants en Sciences

Économiques et Commerciales), you shouldn't spend more than **one hour** on any decision.

And, in my experience, you almost always make the right decision in the end. I think there are several possible reasons for this. First, I think we are usually smarter than we think we are. Our brains are noodling over the choices, weighing pros and cons, and typically come up with the right answer.

Another reason, and I think this is true more often than not; we knew the right choice to begin with. Of course, it's time to move in with her. Yes, we should have gotten married months ago. And the skydiving? Nice try, you have to read the other article.

But most of the time, we know the right answer, we just need to convince ourselves.

And finally, we humans are great at self-rationalization. Once we make a decision, we are pretty good at convincing ourselves it was the right one. And why not? You've made the decision; you may as well make the best of it.

EverydayPower says:

When the thought of staying in your current situation brings you more anxiety than the thought of removing yourself from that state, you know you've made the right decision.

So, if you are riding the fence over a decision, think it through with these points in mind. Make sure you aren't just waffling because you already know the right answer. Go through the pros and cons quickly; you probably know what they all are.

But sooner, rather than later, commit.

Take a leap of faith.

How to Stop Planning and Start Doing

Focus on today and get more done.

Photo by airfocus on Unsplash

Remember that job interview question, where they ask where you see yourself in five years? I always tried to prepare an answer just in case they asked it. The reason is, I never thought that far ahead.

Most days, I can hardly plan past lunch.

But almost every productivity guru stresses that your first step should be planning your life goals. And since it's so popular and pervasive, I have to assume it's important.

It's just not important to me.

I used to have a coworker that was a planner. She could plan anything to the nth degree. Flowcharts and Gantt charts and spreadsheets, oh my. She would spend days, weeks even, planning the simplest project.

I never once knew her to complete one.

So that's what I want to talk to you about today. Not about planning, but doing. Don't get me wrong. You need to have a plan. A roadmap is essential to get anywhere. And every roadmap, whether a fold-up paper map from the Sinclair station or Waze on your mobile device has two components; a destination and a route.

You need both to succeed. But you can get bogged down in the planning. I use Google Maps. And anytime I want to go somewhere and I'm not sure how to get there or what the best route is, I bring up the app and plug in the destination. Then it will show me three or four ways to get there. I used to analyze each route and trying to decide which one to take.

Until I realized I had spent more time planning than the two to three-minute difference, each route entailed.

Eventually, you just need to hop in the car and go.

So, a plan is important, and I think it is important to use some sort of system to keep track of your plans, projects, and tasks. You need a system to break plans into projects and projects into tasks and prioritizing tasks. I've written about that before.

But once I've filled all of that in, I stop planning. I have one view in my task management app that I use all the time. That view is Today. Today is all I need to look at because it's all I can deal with. I don't have a view called tomorrow. Why?

Because I don't need one. If I wait 24 hours, tomorrow will be today, and that's when I need to deal with it.

But I take it further. Every to-do app has some sort of priority sorting. As I explained in another article, my approach is sort of a mashup of other methods, including GTD. My main takeaway from GTD is what's next. Not only do I not worry about what I need to do tomorrow, but I also don't worry about what I need to do later today.

I worry about what's next.

Most task management apps only have three of four priorities. That's not enough for me. Unless I only had three or four things to do today, which isn't likely. So, I usually end up with some sort of workaround. Back when I was using Outlook, I changed the percent complete field to be a priority. 100 levels of priority; now we're talking. I didn't really need that many, but it allowed me the flexibility to put everything in exact order. Finish a task; check it off, and what's next pops up.

My current productivity crush, ClickUp only has four levels, but they have custom fields you can use any way you want. So I have a numeric field called Priority. I don't know how many levels I have in there, but it's enough. At the end of each day, I prioritize the next day. Everything in order. To me, it's not good to know I have six urgent items. I can't do six of them at a time. I only want to know one thing.

What's next.

Despite my warning about spending too much time planning, this level of detail takes a bit more time. But my day is much less stressful and much more productive. How much time do you spend worrying about the fifty things you have to do today? How much better would it be if you only worried about one?

That's what I do. You do you.

Now, if you'll excuse me, I can check off writing the first draft of this article.

I need to find out what's next.

Plan Time to Waste Time

And get more done

Photo by Andrea Piacquadio from Pexels

Productivity is all about planning your time so you accomplish more and waste less time. But a lot of what we consider wasted time isn't really wasted at all. We're just doing it at the wrong times. Recreation, leisure, entertainment, and just plain idle thought, is not time wasted. We need those in our lives. So instead of fighting them, plan for them.

Social Media

I spend twenty minutes, a few times a day, going through my social media feeds. I'm not wasting time. (Well, yeah, I am a little). I'm marketing, I'm seeking out new and productive followers, I'm researching articles to write and photos to shoot.

Outside of the few seconds I'll spend watching the latest viral video, this isn't a waste of time.

So I plan for it. It's on my to-do list. First thing in the morning, around lunch, late afternoon, and next-to-last thing at night.

This is time scheduled for social media. At any point in the day when I am being 'productive,' say, writing this article, I don't have the temptation to stop and browse my Twitter feed, because I know that time will come soon.

Breaks

You need them. Take them. Plan for them. Don't wait until you are exhausted and "have to take a break." That's like waiting until you are dehydrated to drink water. It's too late. Plan frequent breaks at varying times. Like I said in this article, plan very short, but frequent breaks all day long. I break one minute in every twenty. I plan five-minute breaks throughout the day. I take a twenty-minute break every two hours.

Then you need to plan one large break at some point. This is a complete break. Get away from work, have some food, relax and get some exercise.

But this is all a waste of time!

No. It's not.

The time you are not on break will be much more productive and will more than make up for the time off. You know that feeling when you are supercharged and in the zone? How would you like to stay there all day every day? Well, this is how you do it.

Before and After

Before you begin your workday and after you finish your workday, by definition, is outside the workday.

So don't work. Just stop it.

In the morning, you need to have a routine that takes you from the moment you open your eyes until you step into the office. I have outlined mine in this story. If you get stressed before you even begin work, you lost the day.

At the end of the day, the same thing; develop a routine. Clear your desk, your computer, and your mind.

Stop work.

It's time for fun.

Have some.

After work, like weekends, should be something to look forward to, not just another time to cram in more work. If you didn't get it done in 40 hours, or 50 or 60, whatever your workweek is, you will not get it done in 10 more. The problem isn't your time, it's how you use your time.

There is an old slogan: Work Hard, Play Hard. The problem is, most of us forget that there are two parts. If you plan your breaks, plan your downtime, and plan time to waste time, then your work time will be much more productive.

So, roll up your sleeves and get out there and start wasting time.

9 798589 749403